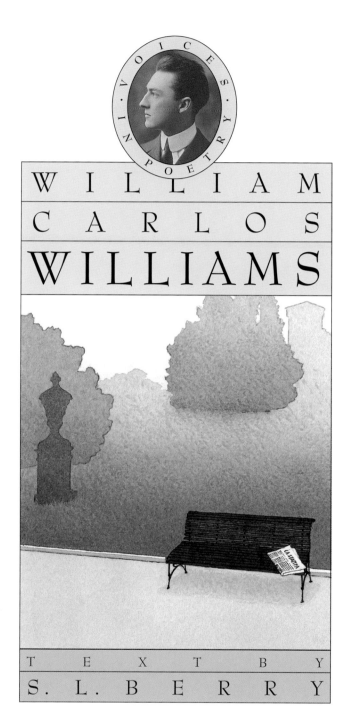

VOICES · IN · POETRY

WILLIAM CARLOS WILLIAMS

TEXT BY
S. L. BERRY

ILLUSTRATIONS BY
YAN NASCIMBENE

CREATIVE EDUCATION

❧ A SORT OF A SONG

*L*et the snake wait under
his weed
and the writing
be of words, slow and quick, sharp
to strike, quiet to wait,
sleepless.

—through metaphor to reconcile
the people and the stones.
Compose. (No ideas
but in things) Invent!
Saxifrage is my flower that splits
the rocks.

From *The Wedge*

INTRODUCTION

"What becomes of me has never seemed to me important, but the fates of ideas living against the grain in a nondescript world have always held me breathless."

—from the foreword to *The Autobiography of William Carlos Williams*

The early decades of the 20th century were a time of revolution in American literature, and William Carlos Williams was in the vanguard of that revolution. A physician by trade, Williams wrote whenever he could steal time away from the demands of his medical practice. His profession fueled his writing, he asserted. His constant contact with a variety of people exposed him to voices and experiences he later transformed into poetry.

Williams believed that American poetry should be more than an imitation of traditional European verse, and that it should be new in form, rhythm, and content. He also believed that ordinary objects, people, and language were the raw materials that poets should use in their work: "No ideas but in things," he insisted.

Williams's progressive ideas forever altered the course of American poetry.

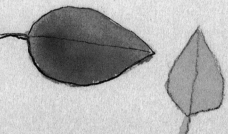

TO A POOR OLD WOMAN

munching a plum on

the street a paper bag

of them in her hand

They taste good to her

They taste good

to her. They taste

good to her

You can see it by

the way she gives herself

to the one half

sucked out in her hand

Comforted

a solace of ripe plums

seeming to fill the air

They taste good to her

From *An Early Martyr*

Born on September 17, 1883, in Rutherford, New Jersey, William Carlos Williams was the first of two children born to William George Williams and his wife, Rachel Elena. A second son, Edgar, was born 13 months later.

Young William Carlos (whom everyone called Bill) grew up in a multilingual household. His father was an English citizen who had spent his boyhood on the West Indian island of St. Thomas. He also had lived in Puerto Rico for several years before immigrating to the United States in 1882. As a result of the years he spent in the Caribbean, William George was fluent in both French and Spanish, which were widely spoken in the region.

Bill's mother (called Elena by her family) was a native of Puerto Rico. Dreaming of a career as an artist, she had spent three years studying painting in Paris before returning to her island home, where she met her husband. Like William George, Elena was fluent in French and Spanish. Uncomfortable expressing herself in English, she spoke Spanish at home and French whenever she encountered someone else she could talk to in what she considered the more "civilized" language.

Bill at the age of one.

The young poet 25 years later.

Bill's paternal grandmother also lived with the Williamses. A feisty, independent British woman, she was the one who taught Bill to speak English. So close was young Williams to his grandmother that she later became the subject of some of his poems, including his famous "The Last Words of My English Grandmother."

Besides being exposed to a variety of languages, Bill was also exposed to literature. He later said that one of his best childhood memories was of his father reading aloud such favorites as the poems of Paul Laurence Dunbar and the works of William Shakespeare. His father also introduced Bill to theater. As the manager of Rutherford's Gilbert and Sullivan Society, William George often staged such productions as *The Mikado* and *H.M.S. Pinafore* in the basement of his house; his sons were usually in the cast.

Bill's closest boyhood friend was his brother Ed. Together they roamed the countryside surrounding Rutherford, fishing and flying kites, playing baseball, and swimming in the Passaic River. "All that I experienced as a growing child and up to the time of my marriage was shared with him," Williams wrote decades later.

Bill's mother, Elena, in her later years.

*T*here were some dirty plates

and a glass of milk

beside her on a small table

near the rank, disheveled bed—

Wrinkled and nearly blind

she lay and snored

rousing with anger in her tones

to cry for food,

Gimme something to eat—

They're starving me—

I'm all right—I won't go

to the hospital. No, no, no

Give me something to eat!

Let me take you

to the hospital, I said

and after you are well

you can do as you please.

She smiled, Yes

you do what you please first

then I can do what I please—

Oh, oh, oh! she cried

as the ambulance men lifted

her to the stretcher—

Is this what you call

making me comfortable?

By now her mind was clear—

Oh you think you're smart

you young people,

she said, but I'll tell you

you don't know anything.

Then we started.

On the way

we passed a long row

of elms. She looked at them

awhile out of

the ambulance window and said,

What are all those

fuzzy-looking things out there?

Trees? Well, I'm tired

of them and rolled her head away.

From *The Broken Span*

Williams (center) with childhood friends, 1890.

EARLY EDUCATION

From 1889 to 1897, William Carlos Williams attended Park School in Rutherford. Later he confessed that he remembered little about this period of his life, except for such extracurricular activities as studying trees and flowers in a forested tract of land known as Kipp's Woods.

In his autobiography Williams wrote, "The slender neck of the anemone particularly haunts me for some reason and the various sorts of violets—the tall blue ones, those with furry stems and the large, scarce, branching yellow ones, stars of Bethlehem, spring beauties, wild geranium, hepaticas with three-lobed leaves. My curiosity in these things was unbounded."

Young Bill's curiosity about flora was matched early on by his curiosity about philosophy. He was intrigued when his Sunday school teacher at Rutherford's Unitarian Church read passages from such Greek and German philosophers

as Plato and Immanuel Kant. Williams was also fascinated with discussions about Christ's divinity, later remarking, "I always listened to everything that was said."

Bill's education took another unusual turn when he was 14. His father was assigned to oversee the construction of a new cologne manufacturing plant in Brazil, a job scheduled to take at least a year. Bill's parents decided this was the perfect opportunity for their sons to spend some time abroad, going to school in Europe.

With their mother as chaperone, Bill and Ed departed Rutherford in late 1897. For the next 18 months, the boys split their time between Geneva, Switzerland, and Paris, France. In Geneva they attended a boarding school, mingling with boys from throughout Europe, Asia, and South America. In Paris they studied French and fencing and enjoyed the sights.

PRIMROSE

Yellow, yellow, yellow, yellow!

It is not a color.

It is summer!

It is the wind on a willow,

the lap of waves, the shadow

under a bush, a bird, a bluebird,

three herons, a dead hawk

rotting on a pole—

Clear yellow!

It is a piece of blue paper

in the grass or a threecluster of

green walnuts swaying, children

playing croquet or one boy

fishing, a man

swinging his pink fists

as he walks—

It is ladysthumb, forget-me-nots
in the ditch, moss under
the flange of the carrail, the
wavy lines in split rock, a
great oaktree—
It is a disinclination to be
five red petals or a rose, it is
a cluster of birdsbreast flowers
on a red stem six feet high,
four open yellow petals
above sepals curled
backward into reverse spikes—
Tufts of purple grass spot the
green meadow and clouds the sky.

From *Sour Grapes*

Horace Mann High School.

HIGH SCHOOL

*I*n the spring of 1899, Bill's father notified his family that he had successfully completed his assignment in Brazil and was heading home. Although reluctant to leave Paris, Elena Williams booked passage for herself and her sons aboard a boat bound for New York. Their European stay was over.

After more than a year abroad, 15-year-old Bill Williams wasn't thrilled to find himself back in Rutherford, and his school work showed it. That fall his parents decided a change of scenery might be just what Bill needed to take his education more seriously, so they enrolled him and his brother in New York's Horace Mann High School.

The first challenge facing the boys was getting from Rutherford to Morningside Heights, the section of New York City where the school was located. They had to catch a train shortly after seven o'clock each morning, transfer to a ferryboat to cross the Hudson River, then catch another train to get to Horace Mann by nine. "It took a lot out of us," Williams recalled years later, "but it was worth it. The associations and the teaching were superb."

Bill did well at Horace Mann. Choosing a course of study that concentrated on the sciences, he immersed himself in mathematics, chemistry, and physics. But thanks to one English teacher in particular, Bill also discovered a passion for poetry.

That proved to be a serendipitous discovery. Competitive by nature, one day Bill pushed himself too hard while training for a track and field meet. Doctors diagnosed him as having "adolescent heart strain." No longer able to play sports, Bill turned his passion for athletics into a passion for writing. He wrote his first poem while recuperating in bed.

Although Williams later described that first poem as "stupid," his effort revealed to him the joy of creation. "From that moment I was a poet," Williams wrote in his autobiography.

PAVONIA FERRY

ENTRANCE FOR TEAMS.

NEW YORK, LAKE ERIE & WESTERN RAILR

ERIE

GENERAL TICKET OFFICE
TO ALL WESTERN POINTS
BAGGAGE CHECKED THROUGH

PAVONIA

The Hudson River ferryboat landing, New York.

17

When I was younger

it was plain to me

I must make something of myself.

Older now

I walk back streets

admiring the houses

of the very poor:

roof out of line with sides

the yards cluttered

with old chicken wire, ashes,

furniture gone wrong;

the fences and outhouses

built of barrel-staves

and parts of boxes, all,

if I am fortunate,

smeared a bluish green

that properly weathered

pleases me best

of all colors.

No one

will believe this

of vast import to the nation.

From *Al Que Quiere!*

*A*lthough he'd discovered what was to be a lifelong pursuit—writing, reading, and contemplating poetry—Williams knew he needed a profession that would allow him to write without being concerned about paying his bills. "I didn't intend to die for art nor to be bedbug food for it, nor to ask anyone for help," he later wrote. From the beginning of his career, he was determined to write not to please anyone but himself.

Williams decided to put his interest in science to good use by becoming a physician. After graduating from Horace Mann High School in 1902, he enrolled in the University of Pennsylvania's medical school. At the time, graduates of academically oriented high schools such as Horace Mann were eligible to take tests that allowed them to bypass undergraduate programs and be admitted directly into medical school. Williams had no trouble passing the required tests.

At first, however, he did have trouble concentrating on his courses. "No sooner did I begin my studies," Williams recalled, "than I wanted to quit them and devote myself to writing."

But he didn't give in to this feeling. Williams's desire not to starve for his art helped him achieve the self-discipline he needed during the four years it took to finish medical school. In 1906, the University of Pennsylvania awarded William Carlos Williams his medical degree.

The University of Pennsylvania.

BETWEEN WALLS

*t*he back wings

of the

hospital where

nothing

will grow lie

cinders

in which shine

the broken

pieces of a green

bottle

From *Collected Poems,* 1934 edition

EZRA POUND

*W*illiams received more than a medical degree from the University of Pennsylvania. He also gained a literary education, in large part due to the friendship he developed with a fellow student named Ezra Pound.

Two years younger than Williams, Pound was years older in manner and literary interests. He insisted that Williams read the works of Robert Browning, Christina Rossetti, and William Butler Yeats. Pound also entertained his new friend with recitations of his own poems. "He was the liveliest, most intelligent and unexplainable thing I'd ever seen, and the most fun," Williams recalled in his autobiography.

Although Pound soon transferred to another college, he and Williams maintained their friendship for nearly 60 years. Sometimes in agreement but often at odds, both men were passionate about poetry and adamant about the importance of altering traditional conceptions of what poetry was.

Early in their careers, both Pound and Williams were categorized with several other poets in a school of writing known as imagism, which relied on imagery to evoke emotions or ideas. Pound wrote one of the most famous poems in that school. "In a Station of the Metro" compared the faces of people in a Parisian train station to petals on a wet, black tree limb. In "Aux Imagistes," Williams alluded to that poem while poking fun at the concept of imagism. Throughout his life, he hated to be categorized.

While Williams went on to form friendships with several other poets of his generation—most notably Marianne Moore, Wallace Stevens, and E. E. Cummings—none were more influential in his life than Pound. Individually and in tandem, Williams and Pound reshaped American poetry, as well as each other. "We hunted, to some extent at least, together," Williams once wrote, "and not each other."

Ezra Pound, 1885–1972.

Marianne Moore, 1887–1972.

I think I have never been so exalted

As I am now by you,

O frost bitten blossoms,

That are unfolding your wings

From out the envious black branches.

Bloom quickly and make much of the

    sunshine.

The twigs conspire against you!

Hear them!

They hold you from behind!

You shall not take wing

Except wing by wing, brokenly,

And yet—

Even they

Shall not endure for ever.

From *Collected Poems: 1909–1939, Volume I*

The Williams brothers before their rift.

Floss Williams (far left) with friends, 1916.

MARRIAGE

*I*n 1909, both Bill and his brother Ed fell in love. Unfortunately, they were smitten with the same woman—a beautiful young concert pianist named Charlotte Herman. Neither Bill nor Ed confessed his feelings for Charlotte to the other until Ed proposed to Charlotte and she accepted, sending Bill into a depression that was deepened by his guilt at not feeling happy for his brother.

This event marked the end of the close bond between Williams and his brother that had lasted for more than 20 years. Although they remained on friendly terms, even Charlotte's eventual decision not to marry Ed failed to renew the brothers' closeness.

To offset his feelings of betrayal and rejection, Williams proposed to Charlotte's younger sister, Florence (Floss), whom he knew had long had a crush on him. Wise beyond her years, 18-year-old Floss agreed to become engaged to Williams, but she insisted that they postpone their marriage until her 26-year-old suitor had time to reconsider.

A tumultuous three years passed from the time Wil-

liams impulsively proposed until he and Floss actually married. During that period, Williams frequently grappled with his attraction to other women, especially those he met in the artistic circles he had begun to explore.

Ultimately, though, Williams decided Floss was the woman he wanted to marry, and their wedding took place on December 12, 1912.

After spending the first few months of their marriage in a pair of rented rooms next door to his parents' house, Bill and Floss bought a house at Nine Ridge Road in Rutherford. A three-story Victorian structure, it was large enough to accommodate their family as it grew to include two sons, Bill Jr. and Paul.

At Nine Ridge Road, the Williamses sustained a marriage that, though sometimes strained by Bill's continuing fascination with other women, lasted more than half a century. Despite his occasional affairs, Williams truly loved Floss; throughout their marriage he wrote dozens of poems with her in mind.

PROMENADE

I

Well, mind, here we have

our little son beside us:

a little diversion before breakfast!

Come, we'll walk down the road

till the bacon will be frying.

We might better be idle?

A poem might come of it?

Oh, be useful. Save annoyance

to Flossie and besides—the wind!

It's cold. It blows our

old pants out! It makes us shiver!

See the heavy trees

shifting their weight before it.

Let us be trees, an old house,

a hill with grass on it!

The baby's arms are blue.

Come, move! Be quieted!

II

So. We'll sit here now

and throw pebbles into

this water-trickle.

  Splash the water up!

(Splash it up, Sonny!) Laugh!

Hit it there deep under the grass.

See it splash! Ah, mind,

see it splash! It is alive!

Throw pieces of broken leaves

into it. They'll pass through.

No! Yes—Just!

Away now for the cows! But—

It's cold!

It's getting dark.

It's going to rain.

No further!

26

III

Oh then, a wreath! Let's
refresh something they
used to write well of.

Two fern plumes. Strip them
to the mid-rib along one side.
Bind the tips with a grass stem.
Bend and intertwist the stalks
at the back. So!
Ah! now we are crowned!
Now we are a poet!
Quickly!
A bunch of little flowers
for Flossie—the little ones
only:

     a red clover, one
blue heal-all, a sprig of
bone-set, one primrose,
a head of Indian tobacco, this
magenta speck and this
little lavender!

   Home now, my mind!—
Sonny's arms are icy, I tell you—
and have breakfast!

From Al Que Quiere!

Wᴹ C. WILLIAMS, M.D.
OFFICE HOURS
1 ᴛᴏ 2 - 7 ᴛᴏ 8 ³⁰
SUNDAYS BY APPOINTMENT.

DR. WILLIAMS

*N*ow that he had a family to support, Williams devoted a great deal of time to his medical practice. Working first from an office in his parents' house, then later from one in his own house, he strove to be a good doctor. He specialized in obstetrics and pediatrics, but acted as a family doctor for many of Rutherford's working-class and poor residents, regardless of gender or age. He also spent several hours every week working in pediatric clinics and hospitals in New York.

Although Williams often complained to his literary friends about the demands his medical practice made on his time and energy—time and energy he would have preferred to spend on writing—in the end he was content with his role as a physician. "It's the humdrum, day-in, day-out, every-day work that is the real satisfaction of the practice of medicine," Williams wrote in his autobiography. "I have never had a money practice; it would have been impossible for me. But the actual calling on people, at all times and under all conditions, the coming to grips with the intimate conditions of their lives, when they were being born, when they were dying, watching them die, watching them get well when they were ill, has always absorbed me."

What's more, Williams saw a vital relationship between medicine and poetry. Watching patients struggle to describe their ailments and their concerns, said Williams, allowed him to hear the poetry of real life: "The poem springs from the half-spoken words of such patients as the physician sees from day to day."

COMPLAINT

They call me and I go.

It is a frozen road

past midnight, a dust

of snow caught

in the rigid wheeltracks.

The door opens.

I smile, enter and

shake off the cold.

Here is a great woman

on her side in the bed.

She is sick,

perhaps vomiting,

perhaps laboring

to give birth to

a tenth child. Joy! Joy!

Night is a room

darkened for lovers,

through the jalousies the sun

has sent one gold needle!

I pick the hair from her eyes

and watch her misery

with compassion.

From *Sour Grapes*

PUBLISHING

While the creative process of writing was very satisfying to Williams, the publishing process was discouraging. His early attempts to get his poetry published were frustrated by editors' indifference to his work. It was only through the intervention of Ezra Pound, who both critiqued Williams's writing and recommended his friend to a few editors, that Williams finally saw some of his poems in print in such small literary magazines as *Poetry* and *The Dial*. Throughout Williams's career, he remained loyal to such magazines, even helping found and edit a number of small periodicals himself.

Williams took matters into his own hands with his first book, *Poems*, by paying to have it privately printed in 1909. That book and *The Tempers* (1913) were filled with poems that imitated the style and tone of John Keats and Walt Whitman, the two poets Williams most admired.

Unfortunately, neither book did very much to enhance Williams's own reputation as a poet.

But in 1917, Williams published *Al Que Quiere!* ("To Him Who Wants It"), the first book to show his true spirit and artistry. It revealed a strong American voice and vitality. Williams had found a way to write the clear, vivid poems he'd been struggling to produce for several years, scribbling lines on prescription pads between appointments with patients.

Although widely ignored by critics, *Al Que Quiere!* marked a turning point in Williams's writing career. Encouraged by what he regarded as his success at honestly portraying American life through poetry, Williams plunged into a lifelong series of literary experiments. In the end, his output was proof of his commitment: over the next 45 years, he published close to 40 books, including collections of poetry, fiction, essays, and plays.

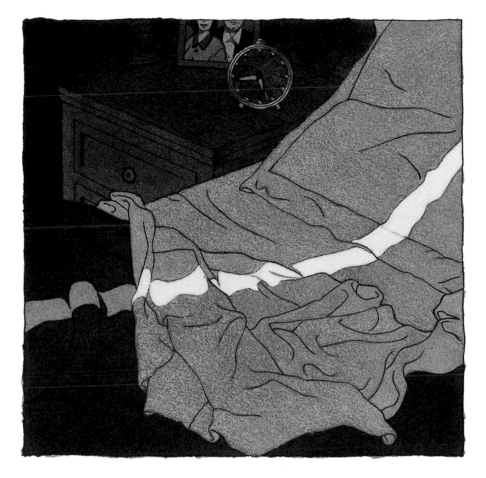

*I*f I when my wife is sleeping

and the baby and Kathleen

are sleeping

and the sun is a flame-white disc

in silken mists

above shining trees,—

if I in my north room

dance naked, grotesquely

before my mirror

waving my shirt round my head

and singing softly to myself:

"I am lonely, lonely.

I was born to be lonely,

I am best so!"

If I admire my arms, my face,

my shoulders, flanks, buttocks

against the yellow drawn shades,—

Who shall say I am not

the happy genius of my household?

From *Al Que Quiere!*

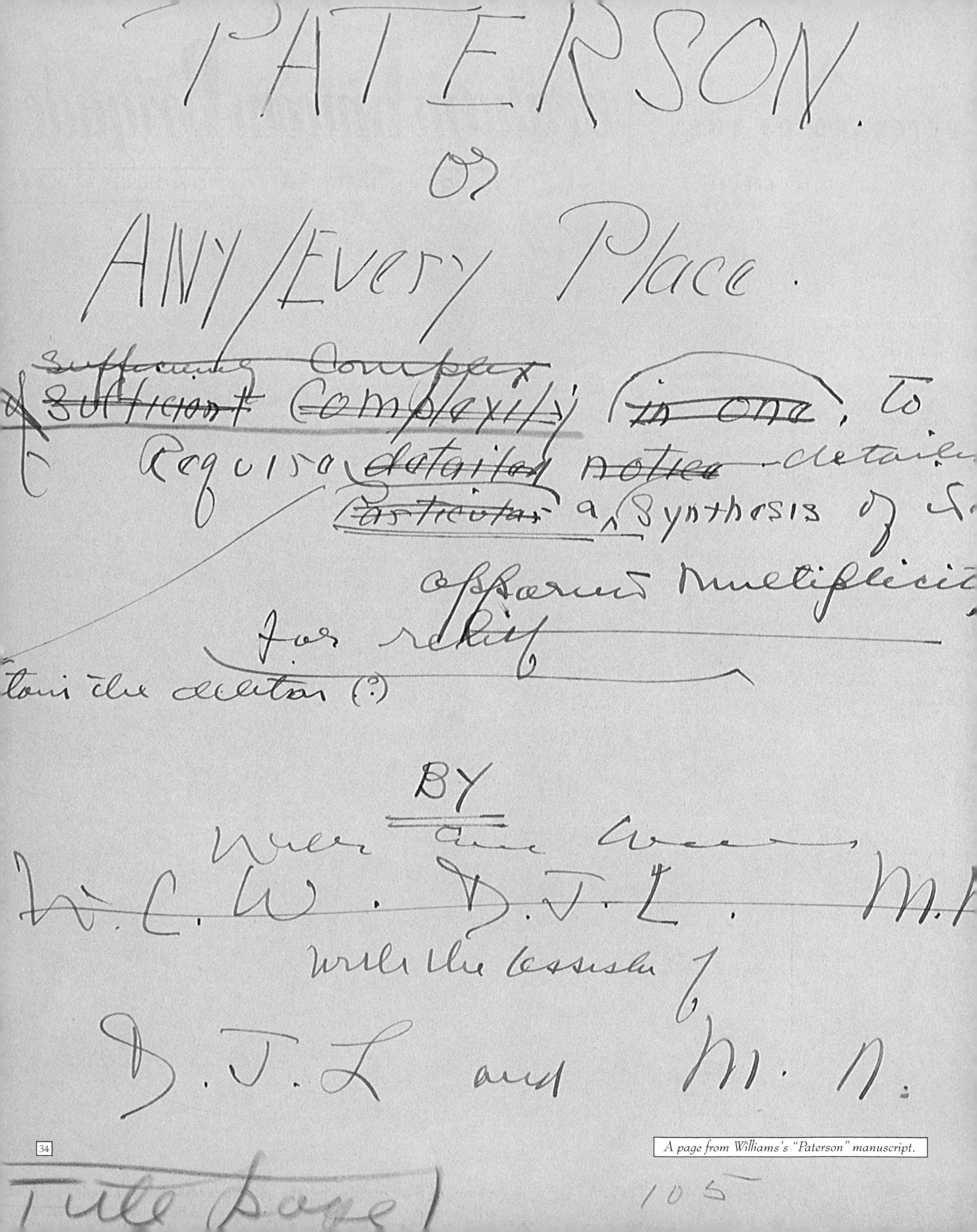

PATERSON.

or

ANY/Every Place.

~~suffering complex~~

~~Sufficient complexity~~ ~~in one~~, to

Require ~~detailed~~ ~~notice~~ detailed

~~Particular~~ a Synthesis of

apparent multiplicity

for relief

from the dictator (?)

BY

Wm. Carlos Wms

~~W. C. W. D. J. L. M.~~

with the assistance of

D. J. L and M. N.:

(Title Page)

105

A page from Williams's "Paterson" manuscript.

As early as 1926, Williams began planning an epic poem that would focus on characters drawn from the ranks of the small-town, working-class people he knew so well. Over the next 20 years, he accumulated pages of notes for a book-length poem called "Paterson," named after the New Jersey town just a few miles upstream from Rutherford on the Passaic River. In writing the story of a place, Williams later explained, he was also writing the story of a life: "A man in himself is a city, beginning, seeking, achieving and concluding his life in ways which the various aspects of a city may embody."

The writing of "Paterson" eventually became Williams's central focus during the last two decades of his life. He worked diligently to create a work in which the voices of real people propelled the poem forward. Early into the project, he experimented with incorporating "found" elements—advertisements, excerpts from letters, sections of historical documents, and so forth—into the text. Happy with the results, he continued to use that process throughout the entire poem.

While working on "Paterson," Williams also perfected a new poetic structure he called the "variable foot." It consisted of lines in which rhythmic patterns varied, much as the rhythms of ordinary speech. The variable foot became Williams's most significant contribution to 20th-century American poetry.

William Carlos Williams, 1926.

*P*aterson lies in the valley under the Passaic Falls

its spent waters forming the outline of his back. He

lies on his right side, head near the thunder

of the waters filling his dreams! Eternally asleep,

his dreams walk about the city where he persists

incognito. Butterflies settle on his stone ear.

Immortal he neither moves nor rouses and is seldom

seen, though he breathes and the subtleties of his machinations

drawing their substance from the noise of the pouring river

animate a thousand automatons. Who because they

neither know their sources nor the sills of their

disappointments walk outside their bodies aimlessly for the most part,

locked and forgot in their desires—unroused.

    —Say it, no ideas but in things—
    nothing but the blank faces of the houses
    and cylindrical trees
    bent, forked by preconception and accident—
    split, furrowed, creased, mottled, stained—
    secret—into the body of the light!

(*continued*)

From above, higher than the spires, higher

even than the office towers, from oozy fields

abandoned to grey beds of dead grass,

black sumac, withered weed-stalks,

mud and thickets cluttered with dead leaves—

    the river comes pouring in above the city

    and crashes from the edge of the gorge

    in a recoil of spray and rainbow mists—

(What common language to unravel?

.   .   combed into straight lines

from that rafter of a rock's

lip.)

A man like a city and a woman like a flower
—who are in love. Two women. Three women.
Innumerable women, each like a flower.

But

only one man—like a city.

Excerpt from *Paterson, Book 1*

An honorary degree for Williams, 1950.

SILENCE

William Carlos Williams spent most of his adult life in pursuit of a single ideal—the creation of modern American poetry. During most of his career, however, his efforts were overshadowed by more famous contemporaries such as Ezra Pound, T. S. Eliot, and Robert Frost.

While Williams was well known within the literary community, widespread recognition didn't come his way until the end of World War II, when he was already in his 60s. Between 1948 and 1963, he won several of literature's most prestigious awards, including the National Book Award, the Pulitzer Prize, and the American Academy of Arts and Letters Gold Medal for Poetry.

He also found himself in demand as a reader and lecturer on college and university campuses around the country. Many younger poets sought him out as a mentor—including a Paterson resident named Allen Ginsberg, who would one day achieve widespread fame in his own right.

All this newfound attention came at a time when Williams was winding down his medical career, preparing to turn his practice over to his son Bill. Yet his years in medicine couldn't immunize Williams against the effects of time on his body. In 1948, he suffered a heart attack that left him weak for months. This was followed by strokes

Floss and Bill during their 30th year of marriage.

in 1951, 1952, and 1958, as well as a severe bout of depression in 1953.

Still, Williams persisted—writing or typing when he could and dictating to Floss when he couldn't. In fact, with more time on his hands, Williams became more attentive to, and dependent on, Floss.

With his wife's help, Williams continued to read and write until 1961, when another series of strokes muddled his once sharp mind. From then on, he could rarely keep a lucid thought in mind long enough to express it. Still, he continued to type. "I'm almost reduced to silence," he confessed in a letter to a friend. "It's hell."

By the end of 1961, Williams finally succumbed to the silence, giving up writing altogether. And on March 4, 1963, six months shy of his 80th birthday, William Carlos Williams died in his sleep.

Scores of Rutherford residents turned out to say good-bye to the doctor who had made literary history. From Italy, Ezra Pound sent his condolences: "I shall never find another poet friend like him."

The legacy that Williams left American literature was at once simple and profound: he threw open the doors that separated poetry from real life. He insisted that they were one and the same, and he spent his life proving this truth.

I will teach you my townspeople

how to perform a funeral—

for you have it over a troop

of artists—

unless one should scour the world—

you have the ground sense necessary.

See! the hearse leads.

I begin with a design for a hearse.

For Christ's sake not black—

nor white either—and not polished!

Let it be weathered—like a farm wagon—

with gilt wheels (this could be

applied fresh at small expense)

or no wheels at all:

a rough dray to drag over the ground.

Knock the glass out!

My God—glass, my townspeople!

For what purpose? Is it for the dead

to look out or for us to see

how well he is housed or to see

the flowers or the lack of them—

or what?

To keep the rain and snow from him?

He will have a heavier rain soon:

pebbles and dirt and what not.

(*continued*)

Let there be no glass—

and no upholstery, phew!

and no little brass rollers

and small easy wheels on the bottom—

my townspeople what are you thinking of?

A rough plain hearse then

with gilt wheels and no top at all.

On this the coffin lies

by its own weight.

      No wreaths please—

especially no hot house flowers.

Some common memento is better,

something he prized and is known by:

his old clothes—a few books perhaps—

God knows what! You realize

how we are about these things

my townspeople—

something will be found—anything

even flowers if he had come to that.

So much for the hearse.

For heaven's sake though see to the driver!

Take off the silk hat! In fact

that's no place at all for him—

up there unceremoniously

dragging our friend out to his own dignity!

Bring him down—bring him down!

Low and inconspicuous! I'd not have him ride

on the wagon at all—damn him—

the undertaker's understrapper!

Let him hold the reins

and walk at the side

and inconspicuously too!

Then briefly as to yourselves:

Walk behind—as they do in France,

seventh class, or if you ride

Hell take curtains! Go with some show

of inconvenience; sit openly—

to the weather as to grief.

Or do you think you can shut grief in?

What—from us? We who have perhaps

nothing to lose? Share with us

share with us—it will be money

in your pockets.

      Go now

I think you are ready.

From *Al Que Quiere!*

ACKNOWLEDGMENTS

Photo Credits
Horace Mann School

Hulton Archive

University at Buffalo (Poetry/Rare Books Collection)

University of Pennsylvania

Yale Collection of American Literature

(Beinecke Rare Book and Manuscript Library, by permission of New Directions)

Illustration Credits
Illustrations on cover and pages 3, 18, 21, 31, and 42 by Yan Nascimbene, from

Antibes, Claviere et Autres Couleurs,

copyright © 1991 by Editions Gallimard.

Reprinted by permission of Editions Gallimard.

Poetry Credits
"Aux Imagistes," "Between Walls," "Complaint," "Danse Russe," "Pastoral," "Primrose,"

"Promenade," "The Last Words of My English Grandmother [Second Version],"

and "To a Poor Old Woman" by William Carlos Williams,

from Collected Poems: 1909–1939, Volume I,

copyright © 1938 by New Directions Publishing Corp.

Reprinted by permission of New Directions Publishing Corp.

"Paterson Book I: Section I" (36-line excerpt) by William Carlos Williams, from

Selected Poems of William Carlos Williams,

copyright © 1985 by New Directions Publishing Corp.

Reprinted by permission of New Directions Publishing Corp.

"A Sort of a Song" and "Tract" by William Carlos Williams, from

The Collected Poems: 1939–1962, Volume II,

copyright © 1938 by New Directions Publishing Corp.

Reprinted by permission of New Directions Publishing Corp.

SELECTED WORKS BY WILLIAM CARLOS WILLIAMS

Poetry

The Tempers, 1913

Al Que Quiere!, 1917

Sour Grapes, 1921

Spring and All, 1923

An Early Martyr, 1935

The Broken Span, 1941

The Wedge, 1944

Paterson, 1946–1958

Pictures from Brueghel, 1962

Prose

Kora in Hell, 1920

The Great American Novel, 1923

In the American Grain, 1925

Voyage to Pagany, 1928

White Mule, 1937

Autobiography, 1951

The Build-Up, 1952

Selected Essays, 1954

Many Loves (play), 1961

INDEX

Published by Creative Education
123 South Broad Street, Mankato, Minnesota 56001
Creative Education is an imprint of The Creative Company
Copyright © 2004 Creative Education
Illustrations copyright © 2004 by Yan Nascimbene
Antibes, Claviere et Autres Couleurs by Yan Nascimbene
copyright © 1991 Editions Gallimard
International copyrights reserved in all countries.

Art direction by Rita Marshall; Design by Stephanie Blumenthal
Printed in Italy.
Library of Congress Cataloging-in-Publication Data
Williams, William Carlos, 1883-1963.
William Carlos Williams / [compiled] by S. L. Berry.
p. cm. — (Voices in poetry)
Summary: An introduction to the life of William Carlos Williams
accompanies a selection of his poems.
"Selected works by William Carlos Williams": p.
ISBN 1-58341-284-0
1. Williams, William Carlos, 1883-1963—Juvenile literature.
2. Poets, American—20th century—Biography—Juvenile literature.
[1. Williams, William Carlos, 1883-1963. 2. Poets, American. 3.
American poetry.] I. Berry, S. L. II. Title. III. Voices in poetry
(Mankato, Minn.)
PS3545.I544W55 2003   808'.042'0712—dc21   2002034863

First Edition
9 8 7 6 5 4 3 2 1